LOUDER THAN

<u>L</u>everaging <u>O</u>ur <u>U</u>nique <u>D</u>onation to <u>E</u>xpose <u>R</u>evelation

Clarissa S. Stroud

LOUDER THAN
Copyright © 2016 by Clarissa S. Stroud
Publisher: Green Cove Publishing
Cover Design: Starvin' Artist Graphic Design
Edited & Formatted By: Tamika Hall, TamikaINk.com

All rights reserved. No part of this book may be reproduced or transmitted in any form or by any means without written permission from the author.

ISBN-13: 978-0692655108
ISBN-10: 0692655107ISBN-10: 0692655107ISBN-10: 0692655107
(Green Cove Publishing)

Printed in USA

louderthanbook.com

What People Are Saying...

Clarissa Stroud has challenged the Body of Christ to discover, understand and grow in the fulfillment of their unique purpose and gifting's by breaking all barriers. Louder Than is not just a command- but an assignment for the end-time.

Dr. Yves Abraham, Chancellor
Eden Christian Institute

This book *Louder Than* will make leadership and the artist take a deeper look on how the arts are being used and encourage them to elevate their thinking and perfect their gift for the up building of God's kingdom.

Lisa Owens
Elder and Arts Director Jubilee Worship Center

I must say, YOUR BOOK, is excellent, anointed, thought provoking! Your writing style provides the necessary tools for anyone to go from one place of being into another - to and for the glory of God! Your book, is very timely, needful and not only should be placed in the hands of other artist but the leadership in our churches! Your book, Should be a required read for anyone who wants to step into the arena of dance as ministry!

You gave some excellent quotes but the ones that I really liked best, were the ones that you wrote! POWERFUL!

Having a book that promotes conversations with other people, keeps anyone from being deceived to think that they have the monopoly in any area of the arts, life and living! We really need each other! But because of insecurities, we won't allow our boundaries to be expanded/broadened, so that other people are allowed to come into our world so that they can receive & not be deceived and vice versa!!

You noted in your preface about taking so long to write the book! I don't think there's anything that you need to forgiven by the Lord for! WHY? Because The time was never to be before ...... BUT right now! You had to grow and be living proof of every aspect of your life being properly aligned to the word and the will of God! You had to go through the years that it took to come to right now, to deliver this word from God to His people. And the final icing on the cake was to become a wife!

I've never looked at you as being a rebellious child of God! I've always known you to want the good and perfect will of God for your life.

So I say it again that, this book was to be completed and delivered now and never before this timing! I rejoice with you and I look forward to the testimonies of how your life lived in the straight and narrow will revolutionize and break the yoke of mediocrity upon the body of Christ in the art of dance! Your book, is not just for Christian artist! It goes far beyond that!

This book can and will touch the life of anyone who has been given a gift, a talent, a skill set, a passion/purpose and it will Point them to the light of forgiveness, grace, mercy, love, acceptance, SELAH, the perfect plan and will of God our creator!

Dr. Sandy Mitchell
Founding Artistic Director of Spirit Wings Dance Company & Studio

Clarissa Stroud has penned a book that delves deep into the recesses of not only the worship arts, but all things spiritual with a boldness and transparency that is so valuable to the church today. The experiences she has gleaned over the years since her youth as student and mentor has enabled her to give a "behind the curtain" assessment of where things are and what is the sure path ahead in Worship Arts ministry. Clarissa is a breath of fresh air as she steps forward to share essential principles that will set the reader on a course that is both spiritually and personally productive. This is a page-turner of the best kind. God has truly endowed Clarissa Stroud with the gift to pour into others and on these pages nothing is wasted in her knowledge-sharing and her ability to get this very vital conversation started.

Rev. Sarah L. Hearn | Missions Director
Evangel Assembly of God INC

DEDICATION

Emma Louise Stroud

Mom, I am sure I will never be able to fathom the depth of your sacrifices and there are not enough words or pages to say thank you for all that you have done.

ACKNOWLEDGEMENTS

To every student that I have had the opportunity to teach locally and internationally…it has truly been an honor to share what the Lord has given me with you.

To all of the pastors and churches that have opened their doors to allow me to bless your congregations with my gift of dance. I am humbled and forever grateful.

Mom:
Thank you mom for the awesome example of strength and dignity that you display. You have been my biggest supporter, prayer warrior, seamstress and my friend.

Derrick:
You are an amazing husband. Thank you for believing in me. You push me to do more and more. Together we are unstoppable. I love you so very much! CDK4L!!

Lisa Owens:
Lisa you were my very first dance teacher. You planted the seed, and watered it and I am so thankful that you have been able to witness the increase. Thank you for laying a great foundation for me to grow from.

Rev. Cedric Stroud:
Thank you for all of your advice and wisdom throughout the years. You have been one of my biggest supporters since day one!

Master's Movement Liturgical Dance Company:
To all who have served in this ministry…thank you for sharing of your time and talent. Your dedication to the ministry has been such a blessing. Thank you for believing in me enough to follow me on this creative journey. I have learned so much from each of you and you are all so very dear to me.

Takeitha Tucker:
You have listened to me talk about this book for two years. It is finally here! Thank you for your prayers and encouragement through this entire process. The Journey Continues Faith Friend!!

Candice Smith:
Thanks for being there Candice. You are a talented young woman and it has been a blessing to have your support throughout the years.

Mentors:
I have had the opportunity to be mentored by the most awesome people in the world. Dr. Ann Higgins and Apostle Henry Higgins, Pastor Yvette Gaines and Apostle David Gaines, It has been one of my greatest honors to serve in your ministries. I will forever be grateful for having been able to glean from your wealth of knowledge.

Rev. Dr. Cheryl Phillips:
You are a dynamic woman of God. I appreciate the level of excellence at which you operate in ministry. I value you and your perspective on ministry and I am so very honored that you would agree to write the foreword for my book. Thank you for giving of your time and encouragement throughout this process. I learned so much from you during our time reviewing the book. I am forever grateful.

Table of Contents

Foreword 11
Preface 19
Chapter 1: Take the Limits Off 27
Chapter 2: 8 Realities 33
Chapter 3: Combine & Create 39
Chapter 4: Wrong vs. Different 45
Chapter 5: Out of the Box…Into the World 53
Chapter 6: Creation & Creativity 59
Chapter 7: With Interest! 67
Chapter 8: Let's Go Fishing 71
Chapter 9: We are Entertainers 79
A Note to New Artists 83
A Note to Seasoned Artists 85
About the Author 91

Foreword

I must admit that for years in the Church, I have often dealt with a level of frustration as it pertains to the presentation of the Arts in many of our worship services. In an effort to "encourage" some people, the truth is often "stretched" regarding their performances. People tell them how wonderful they are, when in truth, their performances lacked luster and were not really ministering to those in attendance. These people may have good hearts, and really love the Lord, but, their public ministry presentations leave much to be desired. Why is it that in any other arena, we expect skill and excellence, but in the Church, we tolerate less than stellar performances?

The Scriptures declare that the name of the Lord is excellent! I always figured that if His name is excellent, and I am His, then, I should be a person of excellence in everything that I do. After all, I do represent Him in the earth. Furthermore, Psalm 33:3 says, "Sing unto Him a new song; play skillfully, and shout for joy." As a person who is an artist, I interpret "play skillfully" to mean that we must also sing skillfully, dance skillfully, draw skillfully, act skillfully, etc. **LOUDer THAN** encourages us to do just that – be skillful and excellent!

For years, we have declared that we were in the "information age." Actually, that time has ended. We are now in the age of "Shifting."

Everything in the earth is going through a shift. New leaders are emerging. Technology has changed the way we conduct life. We are on information overload. Now we must shift! It is time to apply all of the information that we have gathered! It is also time for the Church to stop "bringing up the rear" in its application of knowledge, use of technology and in its ability to access the creative flow of God. To reach this generation requires knowledge, skill and anointing!!!

I have been extremely blessed to have personally witnessed the dance ministry of Clarissa Stroud. Not only is she highly anointed, but she is extremely talented and skillful. (As she should be.) I have seen her grow into an awesome Minister of Dance. Her heart is to please God by offering the most proficient of expression of worship she can present to Him.

As you read this book, know that you are safe in Clarissa's hands. She is encouraging us all to tap into a deeper level of creativity, so that we can produce a more excellent expression of worship to our excellent God.

The late Danniebelle Hall wrote and recorded a song entitled, **Designer's Original.** I want to quote the lyrics to the chorus here:

You're a Designer's Original
You're one of a kind
Created by the Master
With one purpose in mind
To be a showcase of His glory
For the whole world to see
A reflection of His beauty
As He shines through you and through me.

Since God is the Creator, and He created us in His image and likeness, let's breakdown the barriers to our creativity and start creating like never before! Think *LOUDer*, conceptualize *LOUDer*, strategize *LOUDer*, paint *LOUDer*, compose *LOUDer*, play *LOUDer*, act *LOUDer*, mime *LOUDer*, sing *LOUDer*, dance *LOUDer*! Let us take heed to the admonishment, instruction and encouragement in this book and hone our skills. Use the Selah page at the end of each chapter to help to think things through. Make notes of ideas and what God is saying. Step up to the challenge to be creative and skillfully artistic!

Let's present the Excellent One our very best. As we do, those who observe and experience our offerings to Him through the arts will be the recipients of the overflow,

Dr. Cheryl A. Phillips
Senior Pastor
Kingdom Impact Ministries

"If there's a book that you want to read, but it hasn't been written yet, then you must write it."

—Toni Morrison

Louder Than...

So what does Louder Than mean? Trust me, as I began to write this book I kept asking the Lord that same question. What does Louder Than stand for?? I eventually let it go, by this time I had already had three other titles and was not sure if this was going to stick! (LOL) So I kept writing. I truly felt like there was more to the title. Then I finished writing and there was no change to the title. So I kept it even though I had lingering questions. I trusted the Lord would reveal it in His own time.

I moved on to the cover design. If you could see the sketches I sent, they were kinda sorta (not really) what you see represented on the cover today. Drawing is not my gift but I tried and I fearlessly sent the sketches to the designer. When the cover was returned it was just what I wanted. The only thing I had not envisioned was the lettering. The -er was placed off to the side. I did not ask the designer (I may have gotten on his nerves with my numerous changes) to do that. He does not know that I was truly blessed by the design of the cover. I do not believe it was by accident that the designer was inspired to design the cover with the -er off to the corner.

So again I asked the Lord what does this mean? What is it to mean for your people and how we impact the world as artists? One day while sitting at my desk I began to scribble this acronym. I had different words for each letter but they were not making sense. I put my pen down and started working on something else. The Lord called me back to that paper and He gave me

Leveraging
Our
Unique
Donation to
Expose
Revelations

I was in awe. One, because the Lord had again answered me. Two, because He gave me such revelation. I was so proud I could not wait to share it with my husband, mom and faith friend.

So I told my mom: She said oh yes that is good.

I told my husband and faith friend together: They both said that is good.

Then my faith friend(such a blessing to have someone to challenge you, pray for you and listen to you) says what about the -er.

I said well me and Jesus just came up with the LOUD I do not know about the -er (LOL)

Then my husband (so good to have a man that Loves God and hears His voice) came up with **E**xpose **R**evelations.

I called my mom back and she said yes..that's better!.
Gotta love family...

Ever studious, I began to look up the definitions of each word. I have included the definitions below for your review. To sum it all up Louder Than or **L**everaging **O**ur **U**nique **D**onation to **E**xpose **R**evelations means...

Using our initial investment given to us by God [before He formed us in the womb] to influence the world toward Christ. By using the artistic giftings presented to us we can take on the role of agents of change to a dying world. These gifts are individually incomparable but collectively unstoppable. The excellent and creative donation to the world will make Him known throughout the land, reveal His majesty, expose the enemy and display His glory. By letting our art speak LOUDER THAN allows us to uncover the gospel that has been muffled and bring to light the goodness of Jesus in a surprising way. All of this in order to gain a very high return of souls to the kingdom.

Leverage
power or ability to act or to influence people, events, decisions, etc.; sway: the use of a small initial investment, credit, or borrowed funds to gain a very high return in relation to one's investment, to control a much larger investment, or to reduce one's own liability for any loss.

Our
(a form of the possessive case of we used as an attributive adjective) determiner of, belonging to, or associated in some way with us: our parents are good to us belonging to or associated with all people or people in general: our nearest planet is Venus
a formal word for my used by editors or other writers, and monarchs

Unique
being the only one of a particular type; single; sole; having no like or equal; unparalleled; incomparable: without equal or like; unparalleled (informal) very remarkable or unusual (maths)
1. leading to only one result: the sum of two integers is unique
2. having precisely one value: the unique positive square root of 4 is 2

Donation
an act or instance of presenting something as a gift, grant, or contribution.
the act of giving,

-er
forming the comparative degree of adjectives (deeper, freer, sunnier,etc) and adverbs (faster, slower, etc)

Expose
to uncover or bare to the air, cold, etc.:
to expose one's head to the rain.
to make known, disclose, or reveal (intentions, secrets, etc.).
to reveal or unmask (a crime, fraud, impostor, etc.): to expose a swindler.
a public exposure or revelation, as of something discreditable:
to display for viewing; exhibit;
to bring to public notice; disclose; reveal: to expose the facts;
to divulge the identity of; unmask.

Revelations
something revealed or disclosed, especially a striking disclosure, as of something not before realized.
the act or process of disclosing something previously secret or obscure, esp something true.
a fact disclosed or revealed, esp in a dramatic or surprising way.
an uncovering; a bringing to light of that which had been previously wholly hidden or only obscurely seen.

Definitions from:
Dictionary.com Unabridged
Based on the Random House Dictionary, © Random House, Inc. 2016.

Preface

With that said first things first...
Lord, forgive me for taking so long to write this book. Lord, thank you, for the grace that you have given me in allowing me to complete it. Lord, let it challenge and bless your people. You, Father, are the Author of Creativity. I just hold the pen...

This book is meant to be a conversation starter, so reading this book with a friend is highly encouraged. It is the hope that a cross disciplinary, cross cultural, cross experiential conversation will begin and ideas will flourish on how to better utilize and effectively activate the worship arts. It's not meant to be critical of the church but it is meant to allow us to look with a wider range or perspective on what we have done, what we are doing and what we need to do in the future in order to maintain our current position yet spring forward to a more effective plane where we can ponder how we can strategically evangelize the world and gain greater access to those whom we are called to reach.

There are so many questions to be asked and answered. How are we to solve problems, generate new ideas and arrive at solutions if we do not have conversation? Though difficult, these conversations are necessary in order for us to improve and excel in the area of the worship arts. This book is not to say that we haven't done great things, because we have; we can look at our résumés, and signs and wonders that follow us. We can look on YouTube and see some awesome dancing, wonderful plays, and beautiful soul stirring music; however, we have more to do.

I saw the quote that says, "Old ways will not open new doors. I am not advocating for us to throw out all of the old ways, but we must clean out some old habits to make room for new strategies the Lord has for us. I truly believe that the Lord would like to impart new and fresh ideas to us, however, we are so very stuck in our present situation that we cannot hear or receive. Therefore, the world is lacking because we will not release some old ways.

How do we find new ways? Ask questions. Some of us have the answers and we need to share. Other answers are just below the surface and we need to continue to pray and seek the Lord until they are revealed. New ideas are out there waiting to be shared, waiting to be accomplished. The well is deep and will never run dry, there is no end! Let's get in the flow and create!

In some areas we may not agree fully with each other, but we must respect each other's personal opinions. W. David O. Taylor, Assistant Professor of Theology and Culture at Fuller Theological Seminary stated, "We have to distinguish between the form of the material and our personal response to it." It is okay to disagree but do not turn away an opportunity to learn new ways of utilizing the Arts because you do not like the form or method in which the art is delivered. Many ideas on our hearts will take collaboration. We need to connect, we need to unify, we need to share ideas, experiences and thoughts because collectively we are extremely powerful.

So let's begin the conversation. Let's question each other, let's start new thoughts, build new platforms, and identify and tear down old structures that were considered platforms but really in essence are obstacles to progressing in the area of worship arts. This book should start us talking. Let the conversation be about what else needs to be done, what we can we do, and how can we accomplish those things.

It starts with conversation. Let's open our minds and begin to think BIG! It all starts with a thought, ponder it a while. Then surrender that thought to the Lord. Let your finite mind take it as far as it can go. Allow God to work through you and watch what He will do. He needs a vessel....Is that you? Let's start imagining. Let's start thinking. Let's start talking...

God can do <u>anything</u>, you know—far more than you could ever <u>imagine</u> or guess or request in your wildest <u>dreams</u>!

He does it not by pushing us around but by working within us, his Spirit deeply and gently within us.

Ephesians 3:20-21
The Message (MSG)

Note to the Reader:

After each chapter there are, "Selah Pages," take the time to write or draw your thoughts about what resonated with you. It is a safe place for you to refine the ideas and achieve clarity. Be sure to document those "new" ideas that the Lord shows you as you read. Write down the things that you disagree with as well. Ask yourself why is it that you disagree and write down your response.

The Selah pages are there so you can explore your thoughts. You can also pray over them and ask the Lord to give you further revelation.

There are also quotes that are randomly placed throughout the book as well. Do not just skirt over them take your time and ponder them and write what comes to your mind as you read the quote.

These pages are just for you!

My son, give me your heart, and let your eyes observe my ways.
Proverbs 23:26

The highest form of worship is the worship of unselfish Christian service. The greatest form of praise is the sound of consecrated feet seeking out the lost and helpless.

Billy Graham

How many points are there in space? You know that last brilliant idea you had? The idea received so many compliments. The one where the entire audience was left in tears. The one that people were talking about for weeks?

Yes, THAT idea!

Well, there is a point in space just beyond that thought that opens the door to an expanse of creativity that has yet been attained. Open your mind and expand your thoughts...

It is yours by default.

You are an heir of the creator God.

TAP IN AND GET IT!

Chapter One
Take the Limits Off

To the only true living, wise God....
To the Alpha and Omega....
To the Sovereign God...
The list could go on...the scripture says if we had
10,000 tongues we could not praise Him enough.

God is so AMAZING! I think we focus a lot of attention on His deity. Do we take the time to focus on the act or shall I say the *art* of creation? I believe that this focus could lead to a greater release of understanding of God and the Creator and Creativity. Reviewing the book of Genesis we see that it took some thought, imagination, courage, confidence and fearlessness to create the world.

God stepped out on nothing, called out light and darkness, then divided the earth from the heavens. He separated the waters and called forth dry land. *Just from that basic description can you picture a globe?*

If you begin reading further into the first chapter of Genesis, God begins to operate in greater detail. He calls forth grass, that will yield herbs, and trees that will yield fruit. *Now what do you see? I can see a forest.*

God then looks around and uses light to divide day and night. He also establishes time and seasons. The sun, moon and stars were established. This moment here provides **clarity in the vision.**

Next comes more **detail.** God called forth living creatures to inhabit the earth. Then He created Man in His own image. Can you just imagine the earth being populated with animals and humans? Just amazing! Actually, it was *good*!

Imagine if we approached our art with the same amount of thought, imagination, courage, confidence and fearlessness. How much impact and influence would we have on the world? How much easier would it be to share our message of love, hope, mercy, grace and joy?

We should approach our art in the same way. It may take us more than seven days, but we should stretch our finite minds to the limits of creativity. Be extremely bold and creative. Be confident in your faith. Take risks, take chances. What better way to show our love to the creator than to create beautiful and well thought out works of art that depict His wonderful attributes and ultimately lead more people to Him? We were created by the creator God. We have creativity in our DNA. We have the ability to THINK about new ideas and process them in a way that is unusual. Merriam-Webster's definition of creative says, "done in an unusual and sometimes dishonest way."

I like that definition because I view the Arts as a unique way to reach outside of the four walls of the church. I even like the word, *dishonest*. Okay, don't close the book!!! I like the word, *dishonest*, because when it is announced that a dance or play or song is coming forth it disarms people, their guard is dropped and they are in a more receptive place. More on that later…

I truly believe that in the area of the Arts we must begin to seek out new and unusual ways to present our message to the world. As artists we have to recognize the power that we have in our instruments. Whether we are dancers and use our bodies, singers that use their voices, painters, sculptors, musicians-- we all possess a power and ability to reach across barriers and cultural lines to touch the hearts of God's people.

Taking ownership of this thought that we have the ability to cross barriers as artists is very humbling. Just think, there are places that our art can go but we cannot. There are still places in this world where the name, "Jesus," cannot be spoken, but we are permitted to present our art. Knowing that we have so much power, authority and influence we must continuously seek to use it excellently, wisely and skillfully. Everyday, we must seek to learn and sharpen the tool that God has given us to reach His people.

We must never stop seeking new avenues and creativity. This means more classes, more practice, more demonstrating, more teaching. Our art has to speak volumes. There are so many messages and images of who God is, that those of us blessed with artistic gifts must share a clear and concise message about our Lord and savior Jesus Christ.

I like to consider God's artists as communicators. It is our job to use our gifts to speak *Louder Than* the other messages that are being shared about Jesus. In order to do this we must continue to study. We must never cease to be on the cusp of creativity. We must push boundaries. We must stay current. We must stay relevant. The church cannot slow down any further in its pursuit of excellence in the Arts. We have made strides but we have further to go. In some areas we have settled for mediocrity and hidden behind "holy" catchphrases such as, "He knows my heart." "I don't need to spend time in class, the Lord does not need that." "My heart is pure and that is all that matters." And this one takes the cake…"Taking a class will disturb my anointing."

In all my years of traveling and teaching I must say I almost fell over when I heard that one! We must break the limits off of our thinking. It is amazing that we believe that nothing is impossible with

God when it comes to our health, finances, education, employment, etc. but when it comes to our art we have capped our imagination.

Locate yourself on the, "artistic spectrum." When I locate myself I can definitely see how far I have come from when I started dancing when I was 12 to where I am now. If I allow myself, I can see where I need to go even after publishing this book. I cannot rest on my laurels. I think the vision is extended with more learning, studying, observing and growing all styles and genres of art and teaching methods. Doing this allows one to stay relevant and current. We should be further along on the spectrum than we were five years ago. We should be further along than we were just two years ago.

The time is over for excuses. The time is now for excellence. The time is now to speak, *Louder Than*, the chatter of the world.

I contend that the Lord needs excellent communicators. He needs those who can take His message to the world clearly utilizing whatever gift He has bestowed upon them EXCELLENTLY, BOLDLY AND SKILLFULLY.

"You are only limited by your imagination."

-Bob Ross

SELAH

Take a moment to reflect on what you have just read and either write or draw your feelings below.

Chapter Two
8 Realities

Let's look at a list I call the 8 Realities:

1. The church is doing a great job at reaching the church.

Being stuck within the four walls of the church has placed us at a slight disadvantage. Totally understanding that we have the victory in Jesus, I think we have spent so much time trying hard to *be not of the world,* we have not done a great job of getting in the world to activate change. We have lost ground. The Arts will be a primary strategy the church uses to regain footing.

2. We live in an entertainment driven society.

Recognizing this, a strategy needs to be developed around this fact. How can we use our art in an unusual way? [Remember that definition regarding Unusual being dishonest? Keep that in mind, we will revisit the idea of dishonesty later in the book. I promise.]

3. People are not coming into the church.

So WHY are we still sitting in the pews? The question has long been asked what can we do to get more people in the doors? The answer is simple...KNOCK DOWN THE WALLS. How do we do that? With the Arts.

4. We have to get out of the four walls and get the people.

We have become comfortable in the church. It may even appear that we have retreated to it. It is imperative that we get out of the four walls. Yes, there is safety and comfort but our future is secured. We must get out and impact the world.

5. **The Worship Arts is the perfect vehicle for reaching the unsaved.**

The vehicle of Worship Arts has been kept in a garage and only brought out for special occasions. We need to tune up and get out more often. We no longer have to lead with just music there is more in our garage. We can dance, sing, act, paint, and write. It is our job to keep the vehicles tuned up and ready to go.

6. **The Worship Arts must be utilized strategically to reach the unsaved.**

Historically, the Israelites sent Judah first. We need to see how we can revitalize this strategy to make more progress today. We need to be better at studying our target audience which is the world. We have to know how to reach them and reach them effectively. We have to practice the art of listening to hear how our audience is communicating, and speak in a language that they are able to understand.

7. **The negative information regarding the church is spreading faster than the Kingdom message.**

Some people have become fatigued with the message of the church. How can we repackage the message? Not water it down, just repackage it so it is received. Just like our favorite brands will often repackage their products, they go through great lengths to assure us that it is the same great taste just a new package. As a consumer we are cautious of trying the items with the new package design but we take a chance and purchase it. How can we do that with the message of Jesus Christ?

8. We as Worship Artists must become more excellent in the natural and the spiritual as it pertains to our gifting.

We must study and excel in our gifting, know the scripture and live the life. Our message must match what we sing and dance about. We have to be a balanced artist. We as Worship Artists must study both the word and our gift to show ourselves approved.

SELAH

Take a moment to reflect on what you have just read and either write or draw your feelings below.

Creativity: *noun*

Ability to produce something new through imaginative skill, whether a new solution to a problem, a new method or device, or a new artistic object or form. The term generally refers to a richness of ideas and originality of thinking.
(Concise Encyclopedia)

Creativity is something that you can tap into through your Godly inheritance!

Chapter Three
Combine and Create!

Creativity is not limited to a certain group of people. Being creative often times requires you to try something that makes absolutely no sense and believing that somehow, in the process of trying, sense will come. Some embrace this process more freely than others. For the majority of people it is a struggle. Gone is that innocence of coloring outside of the lines, painting with your hands and not caring how much gets in your hair, or wearing whatever you like to wear despite the fact that it does not match.

Finding your creativity may require you to think without fear, and ask questions that you think you already have answers for. Digging deeper into the well of creativity will require you to change your perspective on how things have been done before.

You must release the fear of being wrong. How are we to receive new ideas on how to deliver the gospel through the Arts if we are stuck in a traditional way of delivery?

Go ahead. I dare you to be still before the Lord and ask of Him, "Is there a new way that you would like me to deliver this message?"

We must ASK questions of the Lord. He will answer. This is the first step in digging deeper into creativity. Ask God questions. The thing He says for you to do may be different and not like you are accustomed to but you must obey. By being brave enough to ask the question you are saying, "Use me Lord to speak to your people."

Be brave enough to go outside of the lines.

Our God has unlimited resources. There is no reason why we should compete for ideas, garment selections, ministry time or song usage. Our God is so great…the word says if we had 10,000 tongues we would not be able to praise Him enough. Why is it that when scanning the worship landscape there is so much repetition? We must explore and develop various ways to demonstrate God using our artistic abilities.

Creativity:

"The ability to transcend traditional ideas, rules, patterns, relationships, or the like, and to create meaningful new ideas, forms, methods, interpretations, etc.; originality, progressiveness, or imagination: the need for creativity in modern industry; creativity in the performing arts."
(www. dictionary.com)

SELAH

The definition of creativity states, "the ability to transcend traditional ideas…" are you stuck in a rut?

Take a moment to reflect on what you have just read and either write or draw your feelings below.

"To live a creative life, we must lose our fear of being wrong."

- Joseph Chilton Pearce

Chapter Four
Wrong vs. Different

Wrong vs. Different…there has definitely been a solid box drawn around these two arguments. When approaching this chapter I thought about why the church is lacking in its creativity as we are heirs of the Creator, servants of the Creator and the mouthpiece of the Creator until He returns.

There are many things that can and have gone wrong in the worship arts arena. I believe that we have developed such a fear of being wrong that we are unable to embrace being different. American author, Joseph Chilton Pearce has been famously quoted as saying, "To live a creative life, we must lose our fear of being wrong."

The definition of, "wrong," is behavior that is not morally good or correct, injurious, action or conduct inflicting harm without just cause. The state of being mistaken or incorrect. Speaking or acting in a way that does not agree with facts or truth, not suitable or appropriate for a particular purpose, situation, or person, not right or proper according to a code, standard.
The definition of, "different," is not of the same kind partly or totally unlike not the same not ordinary or common.

I have heard countless Worship Artists say to me, "No my pastor will not go for that." Some of the ideas that were shared with me were AWESOME! My "favorite" response is, "This is the way that we have always done it so we are going to keep on doing it this way."

Let's get on one accord here, there are plenty of wrong things that can happen. I have been in venues where a dancer's pants have fallen down, notes from singers were just off key and wrong, the band was not in sync, lines from the script were forgotten and the list could go on. Working from the perspective that the heart of the artists is not to offend but to express God and His message, I do not believe that it is the intention of any artist to offend anyone. Realizing that everyone's heart is not fully surrendered, I do believe that all artists are subject to experiencing self-centeredness if not careful. Instead of reflecting *His* Glory we deflect it by absorbing some of God's praise. As a result, the Worship Arts Ministry has been held tightly in some churches, unable to function in the fullness of its creativity. In recent years this has changed and ministry has begun to flourish. This is so very exciting to see artists all over the world pursue their calling with vigor, passion and freedom.

During the time the worship arts ministry was held so very tightly, the world was steadily advancing in its pursuit of excellence in the Arts. And the church has suffered-not only in the loss of time but in the pursuit of excellence. As a result, some artists have not been accepted by the church. Because the church did not know exactly what to do. The church was not ready to embrace them. The artists have been limited in their creative ability hence, their overall creativity has been severely stifled. Many barriers were placed in front of the artists to hinder the pure flow of creativity. Many became frustrated and left the church. Others remained, but stayed seated in the pew not able to translate what stirred in their heart through their gift.

In this new season, the argument Wrong vs. Different has to be revisited and addressed by both artists and the church. The church must change their perspective on the Arts and seek to reclaim this powerful vehicle for reaching the world. The artists must pursue higher heights in the Arts, unhindered by traditions or man's doctrine, fully surrendered to the word of God excellently. Understanding that a soul is in the balance waiting for you as an artist to use your gift to fearlessly translate the word of God for them. In order to do this we must establish clear meaning between wrong and different.

Leaders who are called to minister to artists must do so generously and lovingly. This is a very critical statement. Leaders who are called to minister to artists are important because they must be open yet firm to provide the love and support that is needed. On the other hand, artists must bathe themselves in the Word and submerge themselves in classes and practice their skill. This is so that as they pour out, God and His message will exude excellently from their heart through their art.

The church must deploy these artists healed, whole, equipped and set apart to reflect God's glory to the world. If these basic steps are taken by both the church and the artists, I believe that the church may not be so quick to yell, "Wrong!" Because the church has properly embraced and trained artists and in turn the artists will not be afraid to be wrong and harshly judged because their hearts will be aligned with the Word. Then and only then will the difference between the world and the church be fully released and encouraged to operate effectively in their calling.

You see there is nothing wrong with being different. *Different* catches people's attention. *Different* correlates with being in the world but not of it. *Different* is good! Say it with me, "It is okay to be different."

The belief that God is pleased with the bare minimum is incorrect you see. God who is able to do exceedingly, abundantly above all that we can think or imagine (Ephesians 3:20) needs His artists to move, to paint, to sing, to write, to dream, to study, to think, to speak BIGGER than ever before. Give God something to exceed! Give the Creator God something to multiply, Give God, the creator more to work with.

You see the difference between worship arts and secular arts is how the audience receives the message of God and how it moves upon their hearts upon completion of the work. Our art communicates, and we have to make sure that it is communicating the message of God.

Be Different! Be uncommon! Present the scriptures in bold new ways! Be the fresh bait that the church needs to launch into the world. Remember that idea that you had years ago…TRY IT AGAIN! Go for it! You can do it. I believe in you and the world is waiting on you.

Testimony:

I had the opportunity to serve as a workshop clinician in Las Vegas, Nevada. The conference host had made arrangements for an outreach presentation to be held on the strip. This was an awesome opportunity to minister the Gospel. I was in prayer as to what song I was to minister to the people of God. Most were doing the more popular songs. After seeking the Lord as to what song I should minister I heard Third Day's, "Revelation." So, I questioned God. I said, "Really? You want me to minister that song? Really? No one else is doing anything like that. The crowd doesn't appear to be into that style of worship. Are you sure God?"

In total obedience I did that song and I danced to the glory of God. I did what He asked me to do. I received an applause and I left the stage. After I finished I said, "Okay, God, I did what you would have me to do. Receive all the glory and let your will be done."

Not long after I had finished, a lady whom I had never met before approached me in tears. She was from St. Louis and was vacationing in Las Vegas and had just finished asking God why was she in Las Vegas and was missing her home in St. Louis. Then she shared how she heard the song in the distance and came looking for the music and saw me dancing. Tears flowed from her eyes in awe of God speaking to her. The person I was walking with was actually from the St. Louis area and they were able to exchange contact information. What if I had not been obedient? What if I were afraid to be different from the rest?

It is okay to be different. I want you to lay down that preconceived notion that different is wrong. Take a moment and think. Who told you your idea was wrong? Who discouraged you from birthing that great idea? Well, let's release the past, forgive and move forward.

Our Prayer:

Lord, I forgive those that may have laughed and discouraged me. I release the hurt, discouragement and fear. I open my finite mind to new ways to express your infinite greatness. No longer will I be limited by people and their expectation. No longer will I be boxed inside the borders of religion. Lord, reignite my authentic creative fire. Download innovative methods of communication so that I may show the world a larger picture of you.

With a heart filled with expectation,
Your Child

If you believe that prayer you are now ready to move forward.

Jesus, undeterred, went right ahead and gave his charge: "God authorized and commanded me to commission you: Go out and train everyone you meet, far and near, in this way of life, marking them by baptism in the threefold name: Father, Son, and Holy Spirit. Then instruct them in the practice of all I have commanded you. I'll be with you as you do this, day after day after day, right up to the end of the age."
Matthew 28:18-20 (MSG)

SELAH

Take a moment to reflect on what you have just read and either write or draw your feelings below.

Chapter Five
Out of the box and into the world.

Have you ever asked or been asked the question, "How can we reach the unsaved? What more can we do to get them into the body of Christ?" Then we proceed to run down a list of all of our works. Clothing ministry, I pass out tracts, I give to this ministry, I serve on the publication team, I always distribute information cards about the church…I just do not know why they will not come.

Listening to the news as a Christian, I am disheartened by what I hear and see. I immediately become sympathetic to why the unsaved do not come inside. This also makes me even more determined to get out. Unfortunately, the people are not coming in and what we have to offer as the Body of Christ is being washed away in the noise.

I love the Message Bible version of Matthew 28:18-20, The Great Commission…It says, "Jesus, undeterred went right ahead and gave his charge." The church must become undeterred and do what it has been called to do. We are all parts of one body and have very strategic roles to play. We must all play these roles effectively, accurately and unselfishly. I liken it to our military forces, we can attack you by air, land, and sea depending on which is more effective we allow that unit to operate. Each member of the military has been trained and is well equipped to complete the task he has been assigned. When military action is needed, leadership assembles and decides on the most impactful, safe and fastest strategy to take control of the situation.

Based upon this assessment, the appropriate or most effective branch of the military is dispatched. We have seen this happen most recently with the capture of Saddam Hussein and Osama Bin Laden and countless other times throughout history. The church must become undeterred and more creative in how it proceeds in reaching the unsaved. It is time to for leaders to assemble and decide which part of the body would be best to send out to complete the task at hand – reaching the unsaved.

Unfortunately, there are so many distractions and interceptors that prevent the Word of God being heard by the unsaved. It would be easy to blame the world for being a major distraction but, the church has been involved in major turmoil in recent years: fallen leaders, scandalous affairs and false doctrines. We have not been the best Public Relations Representatives for the Lord. Our job of convincing others to join us on the journey down the narrow road has become increasingly difficult considering all that we as the church has inflicted upon ourselves, not to mention the glitz and glamour of the easy road presented by the world.

So what are we to do? Leaders must reassemble and find another approach. Reviewing Judges 1:2 and 20:18 we see that the approach was to send Judah first. As artists we tend to align ourselves with the tribe of Judah. We align ourselves with the "praisers" so YES…a thousand times YES! We should go first!

Now let us take a PAUSE…

As stated before we are all parts of one body similar to that of the military--military equipped and well trained to effectively, accurately and unselfishly complete the task at hand. So there are a few questions we need to ask ourselves:
- How can we go first if we as artists are not equipped?
- How can we go first if we are not trained effectively?
- How can we go first if we are not accurate?
  How can we go first if we are not unselfish?

- If the leaders reassembled and sent Judah first how many of us would really be ready?
- Is there another class you can attend to perfect your gift?
- Is there another book you can read to expand your thought on worship arts?
- Is there a course on evangelism that you can take that would assist you in relating more to the audience?
- Is there more you can do to grow in the area of worship arts?
- Have you studied your target audience? Yes, they need Jesus but have you discovered the best method to reach them?

One of my favorite quotes is, "We live in a Microwave society but serve a Crock Pot God." When I heard Pastor Jentzen Franklin say this on one of his broadcasts I immediately posted it on Facebook. So now the question becomes, how can we get God and his message to the people in an accurate and precise manner in 3 minutes or less? THE ARTS! Send the Arts first! Artistic communication transcends barriers. In this season we must begin to use the Arts more than ever before. Leaders must assemble and utilize this part of the body more effectively. Artists must give their leaders something to work with by staying skilled, relevant and teachable.

TOGETHER, Apostle, Painter, Pastor, Dancer, Evangelist, Singer, Preacher, Poet, Teacher, etc., we must be undeterred and GO!

SELAH

Take a moment to reflect on what you have just read and either write or draw your feelings below.

"There is nothing holding back the church but the church. We are slow to embrace change. Quick to hold on to doctrine. Chasing the world instead of leading it to Christ."

Min. Clarissa S. Stroud

"I will take the hits if someone else can learn and grow. To tear down walls you may accidentally get hit by something else or flying debris."

Min. Clarissa S. Stroud

Chapter Six
Genesis 1:1-3
The History of Creation

1 In the beginning God created the heavens and the earth. 2 The earth was without form, and void; and darkness was[a] on the face of the deep. And the Spirit of God was hovering over the face of the waters. 3 Then God said, "Let there be light;" and there was light.

We must know the Creator God, the one who spoke the world into existence. Not only must we know Him, we have to take the initiative and the authority that He gave us. As we examine the history of creation. We see that the Spirit of God was waiting in suspense to carry out the command given by God. The same holds true today. The Holy Spirit is waiting for our command to bring our creative genius to manifestation.

God had an idea and said, "Let there be…,"and there it was. He had no restrictions or constraints that we were informed about, from what we can see He thought about it and then spoke it into existence.

Today we have so many distractions, hindrances, preconceived notions that we have limited our ability to think in the expanse of creativity.

I propose to you that one of our greatest hindrances as Christian Artists has been RELIGION. Oh yes, the very thing that gives us hope, strength, structure and purpose has also limited our level of creativity. I know many of you are already saying, "No way! Blasphemy!"

Well, before you throw the book down let us examine this further because the key to unlocking new levels of creativity is within the pages ahead. When we look at God and how we depict Him in our art, the majority of pictures or paintings depict Him as a baby, serving communion, embracing children, the famous self-portrait with brilliant blue eyes, hanging on the cross, or ascending into glory. In recent years there has been an insurgence of Lion of Judah and Lamb paintings.

We may use these images to depict God but do these images put God in a box?

My concern or major point is until Jesus returns what other images do we have to show the unsaved? You see, the unsaved have no direct connection to these images. So how are we going to let them know about Jesus? How are we going to let the unsaved know about the awesome God we serve? Throughout each chapter of this book I want to work through, breakdown, and really destroy things and patterns of thinking that limit our creativity.

You ask, "Why is this even necessary? My worship is awesome. People clap when I sing or dance. They weep when they stare at my painting. There is a thunderous applause at the end of my production or spoken word events. Why do we need to do this? Why is it necessary?"

Simply put…we are not doing a great job of representing the Creator God to the unsaved. We are doing a FABULOUS job displaying him to ourselves. Unfortunately, we have not been commissioned to do that. We have done an EXCEPTIONAL job of excluding those we have been sent to save.

As a member of a sorority I know what it means to be in an exclusive club where only those who have crossed through the initiation process are allowed to have membership. You see, we have created this dynamic of exclusivity in the church. This dynamic has been exacerbated by the further decomposition of the Body of Christ. The messages that we are sending the unsaved are dramatically different, often times confusing.

I have had the great honor of teaching dance and the Worship Arts in various venues including churches of various denominations both nationally and internationally. From women not allowed to preach, to the head must be covered, no pants, no jewelry-- I have seen a lot. In spite of all of the differences my perspective has remained true no matter the denomination or statement of beliefs.

Kingdom.

In spite of all of the differences, my **teaching** strategy has remained true no matter the denomination or statement of beliefs. Give your all. Pour out your love to the Father using your gifts.

Excellence.

In spite of all of the differences, my **mission** has remained true no matter the denomination or statement of beliefs. You will do this excellently. Not only because I said so but because the Father deserves it.

Take Him To The World.

We are the only Jesus that the unsaved are going to see until He cracks the sky and reveals Himself. We have to paint a better picture of Him and this Kingdom message until He comes.

When we look at the world, the creative artists whom I will refer to as the unsaved are creative. They strive to top their last performance--bigger and better every time. The world, both saved and unsaved, flock to see their excellent, innovative and spectacular performance. We watch in amazement and awe at how the unsaved creatives repeatedly reinvent and recombine to create jaw dropping presentations that bring glory to themselves and their god.

It appears that there is no limit to the creativity of the unsaved creatives. The unsaved creatives have no fear of being wrong. The proverbial creative envelope is constantly being pushed. It has been this way for as long as I can remember. In the 80's and early 90's we were baffled by artists like Madonna as she produced classic videos, "Like a Prayer" "Vogue" and countless others. Prince just let us all know what was going on as his lyrics had us partying like it was 1999. He held nothing back for us to imagine. Michael Jackson one of my most favorite artists never ceased to creatively amaze me. Fast forward a few years and more awesome performers emerged and again we the church were dumbfounded at how creative their presentations were.

Currently, there is a new group of unsaved creatives that have absolutely no fear. They start at the lines drawn by their predecessors and RUN! In the last few years we have had the awesome privilege of observing fearless creativity. At times it was brilliantly appalling, however I applaud the level of thought and bravery to carry out the visions of the creative unsaved. If we are truly honest with ourselves we have stood in great distasteful admiration for the creativity of the unsaved but not the message.

The truth is, we do not have to stand in awe and admiration--WE ARE HEIRS OF THE CREATOR GOD. Creativity is in our DNA. The unsaved creatives have a mutated strand of creative DNA from the original Creator God. I describe it as mutated because it has taken over and spread throughout the world like wildfire. It is creativity without relationship with the one true creator.

We must DIG DEEPER. I used to cringe at these words, you see I had an AMAZING Bible College professor, Dr. Preston Williams, who would hardly ever accept the first answer to the question. He would politely yet firmly respond with, "DIG DEEPER." No matter how profound the answer, he would say, "That is good but, DIG DEEPER."

Out of obedience and sheer determination to know more about the word of God, the wheels of our mind would begin to turn rapidly.

There are wells of creativity that we have not even tapped yet. We need to return back to the source and tap in and bring to the surface new dimensions of creativity in worship that need to be brought forth for such a time as this. We have to return to the source. I know some are saying, "I never left the source, I stay connected everyday. I fast, I pray and I get in His word."

Yes, that I do not doubt. However, we need to return to the source and ask more questions of Him. Ask Him to download new strategies that we can use to fulfil the commission to go and make disciples. I implore you to be authentic in your approach. You and your worship are enough. Be sincere in your approach. Show your true yet simple love for the Father. Be humble in your approach. It is truly an honor and a privilege to go before His people.

There is enough pomp and circumstance found in the church today. Just give them Jesus through your gift--not a title or credentials because neither can save them. Give the world Jesus through your art.

"God has given us the creativity to win the world."

Min. Takeitha Tucker

SELAH

Take a moment to reflect on what you have just read and either write or draw your feelings below.

Chapter Seven
With interest!

The Lord wants His investment of talent back from you WITH INTEREST!

I was around 12 years old when I began to dance. It was a solo at my Christian School's Christmas production. The song was, "Oh Holy Night," by Mahalia Jackson. My dance teacher, Vickie Wooten, met with me and trained me on the solo after school. Behind the scenes my mother had been worried. This was the first time that I had ever performed a solo and she didn't know what to expect. Well, apparently I did a great job to everyone's surprise and immediately my mother enrolled me in dance classes at Dancers For Christ with Lisa Owens. It was then that my mother said, "My child has a gift," and being a good steward over that gift she invested in it and it has multiplied.

In the parable of the Talents, the owner was taking a long journey and distributing his property amongst his servants. He gave five, two and one talents respectively to each servant. The servants who received five and two talents doubled their talents. The servant with one dug a hole and placed his there.

We are very familiar with the story. As I was reading it again, verse 27 jumped out at me. It is the response to the servant that returned with
just one talent. Matthew 25:27 says, "Then you should have invested my money with the bankers, and at my coming I would have received what was my own with interest."

Focusing on the later portion of that verse we see the owner say, "I would have received what was my own with interest."

I believe there is an expectation of the Lord to receive what gifts and talents He has given us WITH INTEREST. This means investing in yourself, taking classes in your art to perfect your skill and accuracy in utilizing your gift, and expanding your mind and realm of influence to use your gift for the Lord in unlikely places. What if my mother had recognized my gift and not invested in it? There would have been little to no interest made on the Lord's deposit in me.

Just as the Master gave one person five and the other two talents, each of us has a job to do with whatever the amount given. The servant who dug a hole in the ground may have lacked vision, confidence, wisdom or clear understanding of what he really had in his hand. Understanding this, each of us have been given huge deposits and I believe there is more that God wants to give us. Ask yourself if you are a high yield interest account? How are you investing in your gift to increase the value of the original deposit?

Many of us can do more to return with interest what the Lord has deposited on the inside of us. Let's get busy it is not too late!

SELAH

Take a moment to reflect on what you have just read and either write or draw your feelings below.

Evaluate your relationship with the Creator. Are you really connected or are you depending on what others are doing and not hearing directly from the source for fresh revelation? The harvest is plentiful. The laborers are few. Those that are out there working should not be doing the same thing when God has called you to do something different. Reintroduce yourself to the source. "Hello God, it is me _____your worship artist...."(finish reintroducing yourself through prayer below. He is waiting for you.)

Chapter Eight
Let's Go Fishing...

Fishing can be a competitive sport, a casual hobby or a lucrative occupation.

In Luke 5:1-11 we see professional fishermen tending to the daily tasks of their job, washing their nets at the end of the day. After a long day fishing with little success, they received an unlikely proposition. A carpenter asked to be taken out a little from shore so that he could continue to share his message and be heard over the multitude. Upon finishing his sermon the carpenter instructed the fishermen to launch out or cast their nets into the deep. The fishermen responded with a slight hesitation but agreed because the carpenter said so...

Pausing here we see several key elements, let's go back and look at a few of them then we will continue with the parable.
First....
1) In verse one it says that a multitude or a large number of people gathered at the lake to hear a word.
2) Even with a crowd present Jesus was looking for something he could use—anything—and he found it in a boat.
3) The Message Bible says he used a boat for a pulpit.

Rabbis or teachers often gathered a group of students to share a lesson or to teach the Word. Here we see Jesus has sent out a "broadcast call," if you will, inviting sinners to come and experience the healing, love and forgiveness of God. The tactics or strategies used by Jesus were not always the norm. Often times they were rather unorthodoxed. Sometimes we just have to "go with the flow," though it may seem strange. Even in the masses, Jesus found something he could use. It was a boat. An unlikely place to share the message of the Gospel but He went with it. A boat became His pulpit.

Verse 1 says He stood and preached the Word by the Lake and in Verse 3 it says He sat down to teach. The distinction of the posture of Jesus as He was teaching encourages us to be flexible in our delivery of the preached word. Note I said *flexible* not careless and definitely without COMPROMISE.
You see God doesn't need your boat. The message was being taught when He was standing on the shore. He chose to get in the boat because it was there. The boat was there and ready to be used. Are you available? Are you in position to be used by God?

In Verse 4, we see Jesus, the carpenter, tell Simon the professional fisherman, to cast out his nets into the deep. Simon reluctantly says, "Because you say so I will let out the net."
Though it was against Simon's professional judgment, he said, "nevertheless at thy word..."

We can learn several things from casting our nets into the deep:
1.) Launching out into the deep will always involve a challenge or risk of some kind.
2.) Deep water involves the unknown.
3.) Deep water will challenge the way you see yourself and the way you see others.
4.) Deep water will force you to lay down your pride.
5.) Deep water will always grant a blessing. We will explore these points as we continue.

There are those of us who have been doing ministry for several years. God is sending a new voice from an unlikely source to propel you to the next dimension of your ministry. Though it may be against your "professional judgment, " our job is not to judge but to stay close to God. Stay tuned to His voice so that we are able to recognize Him when it is Him and/or His blessing coming through an unlikely source. We have to be so very sure and confident of His voice and His leading that no matter who does not understand or believe, we will go forward with what God is calling us to do. We have to launch out into the deep.

As we continue through chapter five of Luke we find ourselves in verses 5 and 6. Again we see the slight hesitation of Simon, the professional fisherman, but we also see the immediate blessing of his obedience. Simon caught so many fish the net began to break. Simon had to call in his partners to help catch the fish. Deep water will always grant a blessing.

This reminds us that the harvest is plenty but we cannot do it all alone. There is a great work to be done and we can't be afraid to do things differently to catch the people. We have to make a practice of catching people while they are alive. Gone are the days of testimony where we say, "he accepted Christ on his deathbed." What is the use of a dead fish? We have the ability to live an abundant life here on earth. As modern day fishers of men, we are not doing our job effectively by not getting out there and catching people while they are alive. We shorten their ability to live that full life as promised through Jesus Christ. We are doing the world a disservice.

With further reading we see Simon had to call in his partners to help him catch the fish. So much so the boat began to sink. Launching out into the deep will always involve a challenge or risk of some kind. There is a greater need to network in this season and to be open to form Godly partnerships. We are all parts of one body and we need each other. You and I cannot do it on our own. It is time to break down the walls of competition, jealousy, envy and strife. This is not a casual affair. Fishing is a lucrative occupation and we must begin to treat it as such. No our reward is not carnal--our reward is being stored up in heaven.
So ask yourself, "What type of fisherman am I?"

Are you competitive? Are you keeping track of who has the most members in their church? Who drives the best car,? How many invitations did you get to speak? How many countries have you visited?

Are you a casual fisherman? Are you just passing the time of day? Relaxing until the rapture? Is church just a feel good hour…Have you fulfilled your obligation for the week? Have you passed out your one tract? Is that the extent of your evangelism?

Is this a lucrative occupation? Yes, for a remnant of God's people it is. There are those who find joy in saving souls. They unite with other members of the body of Christ, go to great lengths and try various strategies to advance the kingdom because they want to catch people while they are alive.

If Jesus could stand one minute and sit in the next to teach the word, surely…surely…surely we can try a different approach to the delivery of the word WITHOUT COMPROMISE. In a society where our prominent Christian Leaders are falling left and right, we must give a different perspective of this Christian journey. We must show forth originality, authenticity, creativity, sincerity and boldness.

You see, in fishing you need different rods and reels to catch certain fish. No *one* approach works. However, it is important to have the proper equipment and knowledge to do the job. You either fail to plan or plan to fail. Preparation is key. A good fisherman will know what type of fish he is catching. He will understand if their habitat is it saltwater or freshwater fish. What is the weather like? Is this the best season to catch the fish? Where are you fishing-- from a boat or a bank?

We in the church must re-evaluate and re-approach how we fish and cast out our net. Many of us in the church do not know how to properly cast a net. As I was researching for this lesson, I did a quick search on how to cast a fishing net. I was totally amazed at how detailed the steps were to cast a good net. It takes great skill, precision and PRACTICE to cast a net. I encourage you to research for yourself. There is a lot more to it than just throwing out the net. There are at least four steps BEFORE you actually throw the net. I will share just a little of the instructions and then tell you what I received from each step in parentheses:

Spread your feet about shoulder width apart with your right leg pointing towards the area where you are looking and where you want the net to land. (FOCUS on the goal ahead.)

Twist your body back to the left, like you are winding up a spring. (Go ahead and get bent out of shape.)

When you have wound up as far as you can go, unwind your body rapidly, while throwing the net up and out. Release everything (HOLD NOTHING BACK) in your left hand and the net in your right hand. (ADAPT AND BE FLEXIBLE…YOU MAY GET TWISTED IN A BUNCH, BUT KEEP PRESSING.)

The lead line under your right hand thumb should be the last thing out of both of your hands. While both of your arms are throwing the net, it is important that you use the unwinding motion of your body to help the net open fully. (OPEN THE NET WIDE…THE HELP OF THE ENTIRE BODY IS NEEDED…OPEN THE NET WIDE.)

Let the net sink and then pull in the rope, (GIVE PEOPLE SPACE AND TIME LET THE WORD OF GOD SINK IN…SOME PLANT SOME WATER GOD GIVES THE INCREASE.) closing the net's bottom and trapping any fish inside. Let the net extend open over a bucket and remove all of the bait. While holding the net upright, make sure all of the lines are clear and there are no tangles (KEEP OPEN COMMUNICATION AND THE FOCUS ON THE LORD) on the lead line. Repeat the above steps and throw the net again. (KEEP FISHING.)

As I close, I will return to Luke 5: 1-11, we left off in verse 8. We see Simon and the other fishermen recognizing that the messenger of God was in their midst. You see, Deep water will challenge the way you see yourself and the way you see others. Immediately, humility, possibly shame and unworthiness enters in the conversation. No longer was Jesus just a carpenter He was now recognized as the messenger of God. Deep water will force you to lay down your pride. Verse 8 reads in the New King James Version, *When Simon Peter saw it, he fell down at Jesus' knees, saying, "Depart from me, for I am a sinful man, O Lord!"* the Message Bible reads, *"Master, leave. I'm a sinner and can't handle this holiness. Leave me to myself."*

Jesus comforts the fishermen and tells them not to be afraid, and declares to them that they will now be fishers of people. Simon, James and John, sons of Zebedee forsook all and followed Jesus.

Let's transpose ourselves into this story – we are the carpenter and Simon represents the world. How many of us are living our lives so that people will:

1.) Do something because we, OR THE GOD IN US, said so, and
2.) 2.) Leave everything (it may not be worldly possessions but old lifestyles, bad habits, negative friends and relationships etc.) to join this Christian journey?

It is imperative--highly important. The alarm has sounded. We must reevaluate and re-approach "church as usual," and accept the call to be fishers of men, not just collectors of titles and accolades. The church has gone fishing…What type of fisherman are you?

As an artist, you must begin to cast a wider net and let your art speak. Let your art reach. Let your art GO! Reevaluate the items you can change that will bring about a wider reach. Eliminate practices and habits that keep you from expanding and growing as an artist. It is time to stretch and grow and be used in a greater capacity to reach the lost. Do the work that has been set before you. You do not need a title to do. God just needs a few fishermen who are bold enough to do something different if He asks.

SELAH

Take a moment to reflect on what you have just read and either write or draw your feelings below.

"We're private change agents and we go in to minister the gospel that causes people's lives to change or their minds to change. When your mind can change, that leads to a change in your life," she told the Christian Post. "It's not like we'll have an alter call and people will be running around shouting, but we definitely want to plant a seed to cause people's lives to change after our performance."
**-Erica Campbell
regarding performing at the 2015 Soul Train Music Awards**

Chapter Nine
We are entertainers

Historically, the church has changed or shifted at a much lower rate than the world. This has caused the world to supersede the church by leaps and bounds. Understanding that we are in the world but not of the world our focus has to become outward to reach our target audience. For years worship artists have declared that, "I am ministering, I am not a performer I am not here to entertain."

Our target audience, is still the unsaved however, the world, the society that we live in has drastically, changed. Information is flowing at rapid speed. It is being condensed into 120 characters or less. Forty-five minute sermons, unless controversial, chock-full of revelation or comedic do not circulate to those that need to hear about the great God that we serve.

Taking a moment to step out of our holy sanctified pews let's be honest with the view the world has of the church. From the prominent leaders who have suffered moral failures to those of us dressed up in our Sunday Best but refuse to speak to our neighbors or those we pass on a daily basis. If we are honest with ourselves. Yes, they are still unsaved and yes they still need Jesus. How the gospel is delivered to them may need to be reevaluated.

How long have we been hiding our light under the bushel under the auspices of I am performing for an audience of one? Now ,let us not be confused. I dance for the glory of God just as some of you may sing or write music to and for His glory. For several years I, along with many others taught that we *minister*, not perform. While I still wholeheartedly believe this is true, I also embrace the idea that we also entertain.

What is the difference? The posture of YOUR heart. The word says, *If I be lifted up I will draw*. No matter the platform that you take whether before two people, 2,000 people or 20, 000 people, the posture of your heart is what makes the difference. I know you are not here to entertain me, the next Christian knows this too but to a world whom we are called to serve they want to be entertained. We must meet them at their point of need. So go!

Go boldly and take any platform the Lord sends you to display your art. Many of us have shunned the platform and justified it by saying we are not entertainers but ministers. That thought process is old and must be cast down. Go boldly! When the Lord allows you to take the platform be gracious, humble and bold! Lift up the name of Jesus excellently be obedient, and leave the stage. At that point you have ministered to the people who thought they were coming to be entertained.

Remember the, "dishonest" definition...yeah...this is where it fits. Share the message, go under the auspices of "entertaining" and posture your heart to minister. You see by going boldly you then become an agent of change. Some have used the excuse of, "As long as God is pleased with my ministry."

How many conferences have we attended just to go back home and accomplish very little to impact our community. The majority of the time we just want the t-shirt so that when we attend another conference we can wear it to say that we have been there and met, "So-and so."

I truly believe that we have lost ground over the years by not maximizing the fullness of our gifts. Now I truly believe that we have covered a lot of territory. That can be seen by all the conference and events taking place literally around the Globe. My face is advertised on a few of those flyers so when I say *we* I am including myself.

NOT MAXIMIZING OUR GIFTS

We have been doing the same thing for quite a while. If you look across the landscape of Liturgical Dance it has been a while since another evolution has taken place. Now do not take this statement as a blame game. We all get comfortable and comfort feels good. When you are watching a movie and you get your blanket just right and then you realize you forgot to start the dryer and you have to move out of that place of comfort and do what ultimately needs to be done. We have found that place of comfort and we have not gotten up. Unfortunately, it is to society's detriment that we have not moved from this place and become more aggressive or visible in doing what needs to be done.

A shift needs to take place in the worship arts. We can no longer stay in this place. We must maximize at a new level. Shake off some old traditions, old groupings, old methods and press into the new. Revive us, oh, Lord!!!

The shift first begins in our mind. We must begin to believe that though we have accomplished a lot there is still more to do. New peaks to climb on this mountain of Worship Arts. There has to be a desire to want to do a new work that makes an even greater impact on the kingdom. Seek the Lord for the area you are called to cover. Where are your feet supposed to go? What are your hands supposed to touch? Do not seek to be at the latest and greatest conference but strive to be exactly where God will have you to be. Then not only will you be blessed by your obedience but those who are to have a divine encounter with the God in you will be blessed because you have met them and delivered exactly what the Father wanted them to have.

SELAH

**Take a moment to reflect on what you have
just read and either write or draw your feelings below.**

As singers what does the sound of your voice create? As dancers, what does the "sound" of your choreography make? Painters, Mime, Steppers etc., what is the sound of our worship creating? How can you make the sound louder to resonate beyond the chatter of the world?

A Note To <u>NEW</u> Artists

It is imperative that you continue to study show yourself approved and excel to the highest heights in your craft. Never waiver in your pursuit of excellence. Please understand that the newness that you bring to the church is so critical to its continuation and further advancement in the Arts.

Your fresh perspective and knowledge in the Arts is desperately needed in the church. No matter what happens or what you encounter always remember this and do not be discouraged.

Humbly share your knowledge of your craft with the body. Your skill does not make you better than those without as much skill and technique. It makes you accountable to share and uplift those around you to a higher level. Do not water down or lower your standards, command excellence. Believe that you are called for such a time as this. You must continue to pursue God and all that He is calling you to do in spite of any obstacles that may come your way. This does not mean to be rebellious, however, it means to passionately pursue against all odds what the Lord has for you. Dive deeper into the word of God and let the word take over your entire being. Be confident in your skill and in the word of God.

A Note to <u>**SEASONED**</u> Artists

Thank you for laboring in the vineyard and paving the way for creativity to flourish. As new artists enter the kingdom, let us be mindful to not force new artist to conform to what we are currently doing. With the new artists and their perspectives comes new blood, new thoughts, new ideas, new innovations and new energy. By forcing the new artists to fit into the box that we have established, we limit the expanse of their creativity. If we force artists to fit into this proverbial box they may become uncomfortable at a lower standard, frustrated not fulfilling their purpose and leave the church. Their departure leaves a void in the church, we need new and fresh ideas to help us take our art and artistic outreach efforts to another level of excellence.

We must be careful in how we engage with new or highly skilled artists. In an attempt to mentor them or shape them we can do more harm than good. I admonish you to take extreme care with their hearts and souls. Be so very careful that you are not quenching the fresh fire in their belly or allowing the fearless creativity that they possess to go under utilized. Instead, work hand in hand with them, humble yourself and allow yourself to learn from them as they learn from you. Acknowledge that they are a resource and stay teachable. Determine to be blessed and not let the spirit of intimidation, jealousy or inferiority creep into your heart or your ministry.
Recognizing that the new artist does not know everything that the seasoned artist does and the seasoned artist does not know everything that the new artist does. We have to begin to work together and combine all of our resources and knowledge for maximum impact and reach.

Our collective goal is to lift up the name of Jesus so that people can be drawn to Him and Him only. Let us begin to lay aside emotions, traditions, schools of thought, or organizations that keep us from uniting to advance and possess more territory for the kingdom. Together we can lift up the name of Jesus higher and unite to share the message of God's love, joy, hope and mercy to the world but first, we must learn to extend that same love, joy, hope and mercy to each other.

Worship Arts Ministries must think outside the box. SHIFT! Move outside of the religious, mental, limiting box that has deceivingly stunted our ability to tap into deeper wells of Creativity. Get outside of the box to become more excellent, skilled and effective at sharing the gospel through the vehicle of the Arts. We must use our art to speak LOUDER THAN the things of the world.

#LouderThan 2014
#artspeaksvolumes
Min. Clarissa S. Stroud
2014 Facebook Post

Here we go.

Okay. Here we go.
We, meaning you and me JESUS.
Guide every step.
Move through me please
Chasse, chaine, pique…
I bow before thee
Tombe, pas de bourre…
I pray, oh I pray that you would use me.
Layout, chaine, port de bra, pause, pause, pause…
You amaze me Lord.
Plie, contract, roll, hinge…
You glory overwhelms me.
 Pirouette, develope stretch to the tendue…
Father I stretch my hands to thee.
Fan Kick, pencil turn, lunge…
I cry holy, holy, holy.
Flatback, Promenade, Penche
With strength and grace I will do your will
Battement, Battement,chaine, chaine fall to the floor breathe…
Step up left, step up right, slowly lift the
chest…
My soul rejoices in thee.
WHAT? No more music? It's over? Really?
WOW…you did it again Jesus…Thank you…

Pardon me.

Pardon me.

Yes you.

Come talk to me.

Yes…me.

I have no appointment or credentials.

Tell me what it is you do better ye*t SHOW ME* because what I hear already is so confusing.

PRESENT something different because what I am hearing and seeing is not making sense.

DEMONSTRATE to me the message you speak of.

SPEAK LOUDER so that I may understand beyond the static and chatter of this world.

PAINT out a clear picture of your God and the message of His Love.

SING from the rafters of His greatness and all the marvelous things He has done for you.

DANCE about with great joy right where you are in praise and adoration to the one you proclaim can save and deliver me.

I beg of you. I plead.

SHOW ME something different.

SKETCH out another image for me because what hear and see are not the same.

Pardon me for speaking out of turn.

I have no appointment or credentials.

I just need you and your God to be louder than what I already hear.

We do not merely want to see beauty, though, God knows, even that is bounty enough. We want something else which can hardly be put into words—to be united with the beauty we see, to pass into it, to receive it into ourselves, to bathe in it, to become part of it.
C. S. Lewis
—The Weight of Glory

ABOUT THE AUTHOR

"The dance movements are honest, true ,and sincere. When you dance ,it is as if you are using your body to speak to God for all in attendance .

The congregation reacts in agreement; our spirits say "Yes! That's how I would want to say it! Thanks for saying it for me!" It is a poetic, yet sermonic moment that connects us as a body of believers with our Maker."
~Rev. Cedric M. Stroud

Clarissa Stroud-Kemp knew at an early age that she had a mission. From the first time she stepped foot onstage as a child, dance has been her way of communication – and the young artist has a lot to say. A professional dancer, speaker and author based in Maryland, Stroud-Kemp has built her entire career around the Lord's word. And her main goal is to help others experience His power, and to show the world the authentic picture of God through her work.

"My mother recognized it was something I was gifted to do," explains Stroud-Kemp. "I literally would take dance classes and come and teach everything I learned to the dance ministry at church."

Performing for the first time at a grade school Christmas play, her mother instantly recognized her daughter's God-given talent and enrolled her in dance class. Studying at prestigious studios such as Joy of Motion, Christian Dance Academy, Broadway Dance Center, and the Kennedy Center/Dance Theatre of Harlem Community Residence Program, Stroud-Kemp honed her skills in ballet, modern, tap and jazz. As she gained more experience, her love for liturgical dance strengthened, and so did her relationship with God.

Over the years, Stroud-Kemp's faith hasn't only made her a master performer, but a savvy entrepreneur. Actively speaking at workshops, conferences, and residencies around the country, she's also taught internationally in places such as London, Bermuda, Trinidad, Bahamas and more, and has done extensive missionary work. She started the Master's Movement Liturgical Dance Company, a program that encourages others to enter His presence through concerts and community outreach. She also hosts the Live. Move. Be. Worship Arts Podcast, which helps artists give voice to their work and provides a platform for them to share their expertise.

On the web:

facebook.com/clarissastroud
twitter @ClarissaStroud
youtube.com/MastersMovement

What others have said about
Clarissa S. Stroud & Master's Movement

"Strong, powerful, anointing and beautiful."

"Loved it! I have seen Master's Movement Liturgical Dance Company dance in person and they have a tremendous ministry! You feel the anointing of the service each time."

"I view ministries of dance quite often on YouTube, however this presentation is by far one of the most sincere, anointed and awesome dances I have viewed. God must be well pleased that you have used your gift in a most holy way."

"There are not many who GET this MINISTRY! You GET it! ...and it is a breath of life sustaining air. Sometimes I feel like throwing in the towel, but ministries like yours remind me that God ALWAYS has a remnant and I don't mind being in the remnant! Some think because they have talent, they don't need the anointing. You are a perfect mixture of the anointing and talent. Duet 1:11 be unto you! "

"Oh my God this is an amazing gift surely every good and perfect gift comes from above you blessed my heart a billion times and I thank God for you"

"ANOINTED!!!!!! When you can feel the presence of God and enter into worship from a video on a computer: HIS PRESENCE AMAZES ME. PEACE AND BLESSINGS TO YOU AS YOU CONTINUE IN MINISTRY!!!! "

"Jesus! That was the best measure of worship I've seen in a long while. Your job is almost done when your ministry can be seen on the Internet and the saints can jump and holler. Your anointing is jumping off of screen! This has blessed me! Thank you.

"Awesome, Awesome, the power of God is truly on this ministry. I always look for the anointing and My God you have it. Be Encouraged! "

"I would just like to say how deeply blessed I was. I myself danced for the lord but moved away from church, experiencing the anointing from each dance has really inspired me. For the first time in a long time I danced before God in my bedroom. Your ministry has done that. Keep up the good work. More of our dance ministry should be more anointed because truly it's the anointing that destroys yokes."

TO GOD BE ALL THE GLORY!

www.ingramcontent.com/pod-product-compliance
Lightning Source LLC
Chambersburg PA
CBHW071730040426
42446CB00011B/2304